# SANKOFA
## BLACK HERITAGE COLLECTION

# RIGHTS AND EQUALITY

## TISHA NELSON

### SERIES EDITOR • TOM HENDERSON

**Rubicon**
**www.rubiconpublishing.com**

Associate Publisher: Amy Land
Project Editor: Jessica Rose
Senior Editor: Danielle Tardif
Creative Director: Jennifer Drew
Lead Designer: Sherwin Flores
Graphic Designers: Roy Casim, Megan Little

15 16 17 18 19    5 4 3 2 1

ISBN: 978-1-77058-828-8

*Printed in China*

# CONTENTS

# RIGHTS *and* EQUALITY

The *Canadian Charter of Rights and Freedoms* became law in 1982. Before that, some people had to fight to have the same rights as other citizens in Canada. Even today, cases of discrimination are fought in the courts.

Social justice activists are people who push governments, organizations, and other people to treat everyone fairly and equally. However, making Canada a better country is everyone's responsibility. What can you do? Read on to find out.

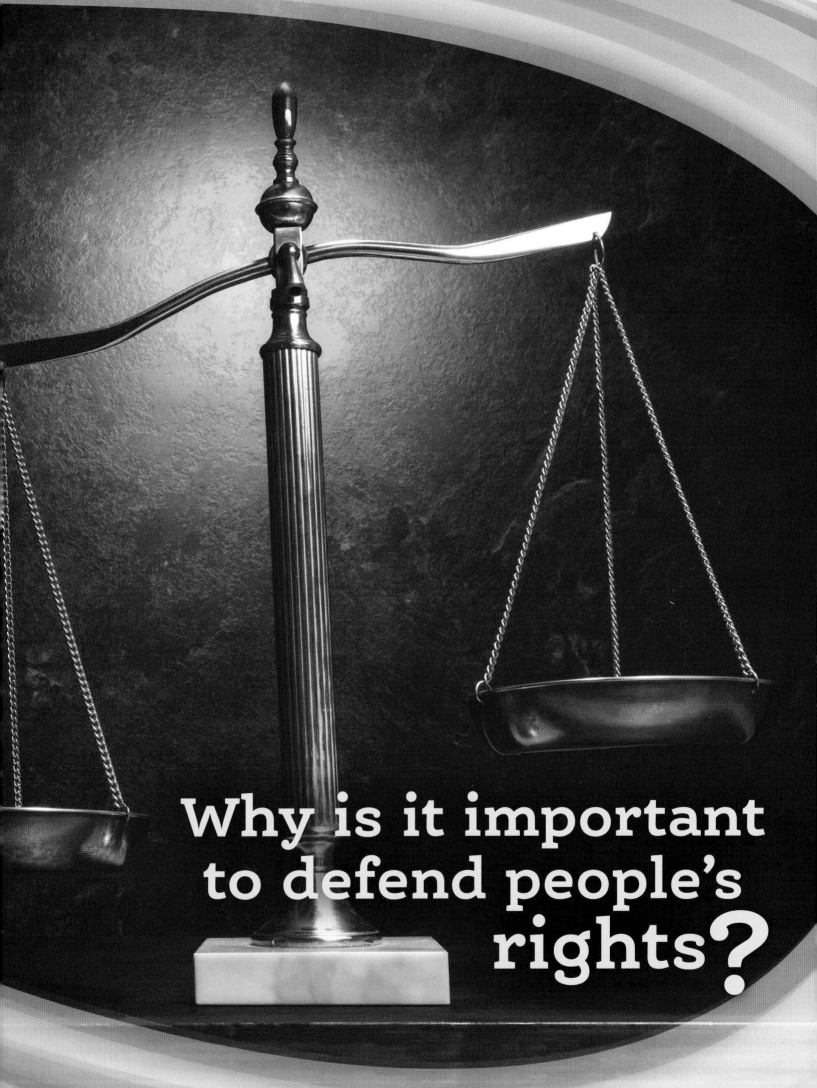

# Why is it important to defend people's rights?

# RIGHTS FOR ALL

**THINK ABOUT IT**

What rights do you think you should have as a young Canadian citizen?

**EVERY PERSON LIVING** in Canada has certain rights and freedoms. The *Canadian Charter of Rights and Freedoms* guarantees this by law. Knowing, enjoying, and respecting these rights and freedoms is an important part of being Canadian. However, in the past, not all Canadians had equal rights. Some people have had to fight for them. Learning about the fight for equal rights helps us understand why many of today's laws exist. It helps us to protect our rights in the future.

Read the following Q&A to learn about the rights all Canadians have and the struggle for rights around the world.

## What are civil rights and freedoms?

Civil rights and freedoms are the legal rights that people have as citizens of a country. Citizens of a democracy such as Canada elect the government. It is the elected government that passes laws to protect the rights of its citizens. Some Canadian civil rights are the right to vote, the right to leave and enter the country, and the right to communicate in either English or French with government head offices. Some Canadian freedoms are the freedom of thought, belief, opinion, and expression. Freedom of conscience and religion are other important freedoms. These rights and freedoms are guaranteed by the *Canadian Charter of Rights and Freedoms*.

## What is the *Canadian Charter of Rights and Freedoms*?

The *Canadian Charter of Rights and Freedoms* is a document that outlines the rights and freedoms of Canadians. The Charter guarantees that these rights and freedoms are protected by law.

## What did the enactment of the *Canadian Charter of Rights and Freedoms* mean for African Canadians and other racialized groups in Canada?

The Charter helped to reduce racial discrimination experienced by African Canadians and other racialized groups, who were often treated unfairly by the government and by the public. Though the Charter has not completely eliminated discrimination against these groups, it helps protect all Canadians against unethical treatment such as unreasonable searches, unlawful arrests and imprisonment, and unfair trials.

---

conscience: *part of the mind that judges whether something is right or wrong*

racialized: *given a racial identity that is neither Caucasian nor Aboriginal*

## What should someone do if his or her Charter rights and freedoms have been denied?

If someone believes his or her Charter rights and freedoms have been denied, that person can fight this violation in court. If the court determines that rights have been violated, it has the ability to correct the situation. For example, if a person is charged with an offence, but was denied the right to a trial within a reasonable amount of time, the court can stop the legal action against that person.

## What is the role of civil rights leaders?

Civil rights leaders are people who speak out against political injustices. They promote equal rights for all. Civil rights leaders mobilize people for action through many forms of protest. They often lobby governments to change or create laws to protect the civil rights and freedoms of all members of a community. Some well-known Canadian civil rights leaders were Carrie Best and Charles Roach.

## What was the American Civil Rights Movement?

The American Civil Rights Movement was an organized effort by African Americans to fight for equal rights for all Americans. The movement represented a mass non-violent protest against racial discrimination and segregation in the United States. The height of the movement occurred in the 1950s and 1960s. African Americans and their supporters fought for the rights of all people who were discriminated against in the United States. They fought to put an end to segregation in public places and to put a stop to racial discrimination in places such as schools and workplaces.

lobby: *try to influence decision-makers*
segregation: *practice of keeping racial groups separate from one another*

In May 1963, young African American demonstrators march in Birmingham, Alabama, as part of the American Civil Rights Movement.

## What are human rights?

Human rights are rights that all people are entitled to have. According to the United Nations *Universal Declaration of Human Rights*, "All human beings are born free and equal in dignity and rights." Human rights cannot be taken away. However, there can be exceptions to this, such as when a person breaks a law. International human rights laws require governments to treat individuals in a way that ensures that their human rights are protected. An example of a human right is the right to get an education.

## What was Apartheid?

Apartheid was a system of racial segregation created by the South African government. It lasted from 1948 to 1991. The word "Apartheid" means apartness in Afrikaans, a language spoken in South Africa. Under Apartheid, South Africans were classified into four groups: Black, Coloured, Indian, and White. Within this system, people were restricted to working, living, and using facilities only in areas that were designated for their race. Contact between White and non-White citizens was also limited. This system of legal racial segregation was finally dissolved in 1991 after years of struggle.

The entrance to the Apartheid Museum in Johannesburg, South Africa, gives visitors an insight into the life of non-White South Africans during Apartheid. To replicate the experience that non-White South Africans used to have, visitors are randomly issued a ticket that indicates if they are White or non-White, and they must use the appropriate entrance.

## CONNECT IT

Research online or at the library to learn more about Apartheid. Then, write a one-page paper about how your daily life would be different if this system were imposed upon you.

# KEY MOMENTS IN
# CANADA'S CIVIL

## THINK ABOUT IT

Timelines identify important events that have happened over a period of time. What are five events from your own life that you would include on a timeline?

**READ THIS TIMELINE** to learn more about moments in Canada's civil rights history that helped make it the country it is today.

### 8 November 1946

In Nova Scotia, Viola Desmond is arrested at a movie theatre and put in jail after she refuses to move from a seat that is reserved for White people. In court, she loses her case, but her struggle helps to inspire many other Canadians to fight for equal rights in Canada.

### 1 August 1834

The *Act for the Abolition of Slavery throughout the British Colonies* goes into effect. It officially ends slavery in Canada and other British colonies.

### 1 April 1947

Saskatchewan becomes the first province in Canada to introduce a *Bill of Rights*. This bill outlaws discrimination based on race and religion in the workplace, in owning and occupying property, and in accessing public places.

**1834** **1944** **1946** **1947** **1947**

### 14 March 1944

Ontario passes the *Racial Discrimination Act*. It makes the publication or display of any racially discriminatory sign or symbol illegal on buildings, on pieces of land, in newspapers, and on the radio.

### 1947

The *Provincial Elections Act Amendment Act* gives the right to vote to all Canadian citizens except for Canadian citizens of Japanese or Aboriginal descent. However, the act takes the right away from some religious groups who were previously allowed to vote, unless they have served in the armed forces.

Under the *Indian Act*, Aboriginal people did have the right to vote. In order to vote, they were forced to give up their Indian Status and Aboriginal identity, including any rights they had under the *Indian Act*.

# RIGHTS HISTORY

## 1948

The federal *Elections Act* eliminates race as grounds for exclusion from voting in federal elections. Racialized groups are given the right to vote in federal elections, although Aboriginal peoples are not.

## 12 June 1951

The Northwest Territories becomes the last of Canada's provinces and territories to grant women the right to vote.

### THE CANADA FAIR EMPLOYMENT PRACTICES ACT
### PROHIBITS DISCRIMINATION
### IN EMPLOYMENT

**THE PURPOSE OF THE ACT,** which came into effect in July, 1953, is to protect workers against discrimination in employment and in trade union membership on the grounds of RACE, RELIGION, COLOUR or NATIONAL ORIGIN.

**THE ACT APPLIES TO** employers in works or undertakings under federal jurisdiction and to trade unions representing persons employed therein. These undertakings include shipping, navigation, railways, canals, telegraphs, aerodromes, airlines, federal crown corporations, banking, radio and television broadcasting, as well as works or undertakings that have been de-

against an employee because of his RACE, RELIGION, COLOUR or NATIONAL ORIGIN. An employer is also forbidden to use an employment agency which practices such discrimination, or to publish employment advertising which is discriminatory, or to use discriminatory questions, written or oral, in connection with applications for employment.

**THE ACT ALSO FORBIDS** discriminatory action by trade unions in regard to union membership or employment on the grounds of RACE, RELIGION, COLOUR or NATIONAL ORIGIN.

## 1953

Canada passes the *Fair Employment Practices Act*, which makes discrimination on the basis of race, religion, colour, or national origin illegal in employment practices.

---

**1948** • **1948** • **1951** **1953** • • **1954**

---

## 10 December 1948

Canada and other countries that are members of the United Nations sign the *Universal Declaration of Human Rights*. This document promotes respect for human rights among members of the United Nations.

## 6 April 1954

The *Fair Accommodation Practices Act* passes in Ontario. This makes it illegal to refuse accommodation or services to someone because of his or her race, religion, colour, or national origin. Ontario is one of the first provinces to have a law of this type. It lays the groundwork for similar laws across Canada.

*Prime Minister Pierre Trudeau*

## 8 October 1971

Prime Minister Pierre Trudeau introduces the *Multiculturalism Policy of Canada*, which guarantees all Canadians "equality before the law and equality of opportunity" regardless of their origin. The policy affirms the value and dignity of all Canadian citizens and the belief that all citizens are equal.

## 1960

Aboriginal peoples achieve the right to vote in Canadian federal elections.

## 19 January 1962

Immigration practices that exclude people based on their race, skin colour, or nationality are removed from Canada's immigration policy.

**1960**   **1960**   **1962**   **1970**   **1971**

## 10 August 1960

Prime Minister John Diefenbaker introduces the *Canadian Bill of Rights*. It is the first federal declaration on human rights in Canada. This bill states that all Canadians, without discrimination, have certain rights and freedoms. These include the right to equal protection under the law and the freedom of religion and speech.

## 1970

The *Criminal Code* defines the types of crimes in Canada and the possible punishment a person may face if a crime is committed. The *Criminal Code* makes it illegal to say hateful things in public about a person based on his or her race, skin colour, religion, or ethnicity.

*Governor General Michaëlle Jean delivers the Speech from the Throne in the Senate Chamber in Ottawa.*

## 4 May 1992

In Toronto, Ontario, a violent protest, often referred to as the Yonge Street Riot, breaks out after acquittals in the Rodney King trial in Los Angeles and after recent police shootings of Black men in the Toronto region. This riot leads to the expansion of the province's anti-racism department, the introduction of employment equity legislation, and an increase in funding for community development projects.

acquittals: *judgments that find people not guilty of a crime*

## 17 April 1982

The *Canadian Charter of Rights and Freedoms* is passed by the Canadian government. The Charter outlines the rights and freedoms that all Canadians have and guarantees them by law.

## 27 September 2005

Michaëlle Jean becomes Governor General of Canada. For the first time ever, a Canadian of African descent is the person who approves which bills from Parliament get made into laws.

**1982    1986    1992    1997    2005**

## 27 June 1986

The federal government passes the *Employment Equity Act*. This act requires crown corporations and privately owned companies that are regulated by the federal government to eliminate unnecessary barriers that limit work opportunities for some people. These people are "women, Aboriginal peoples, persons with disabilities, and members of visible minorities."

crown corporations: *organizations that are structured like private or independent companies but are owned by the government*

## 1997

The Canadian Race Relations Foundation opens its doors. This organization's main goals are to end racism and to promote racial harmony among Canadians.

## CONNECT IT

Many other events in history have contributed to Canada's identity. Find another civil rights event that changed Canada. Write a short summary about this event.

# STRIVE TO BE LIKE ROSA

## BY CHARLES ROACH

## THINK ABOUT IT

The poet Charles Roach believes that all people can bring about change. Discuss with a classmate why you agree or disagree with this statement.

**CHARLES ROACH USED** his poetry to inform, motivate, and mobilize people in the fight for justice. "Strive to Be Like Rosa" is a poem about Rosa Parks, an African American woman who refused to give up her seat on a bus to a White man in 1955.

Charles Roach

## ABOUT THE POET

Charles Roach was born in Trinidad and Tobago. He came to Canada in 1955, and he began his work as a civil rights lawyer and human rights advocate. He urged African Canadians to run for public office and to fight racism and inequality. He also co-founded Caribana, which is now known as the Scotiabank Caribbean Carnival Toronto.

Roach is most famous for trying to become a Canadian citizen without swearing an oath to the Queen. He believed that having to swear an oath to a monarch violated his rights under the *Canadian Charter of Rights and Freedoms*. After fighting this battle for 24 years, Roach died at the age of 79, never having become a Canadian citizen.

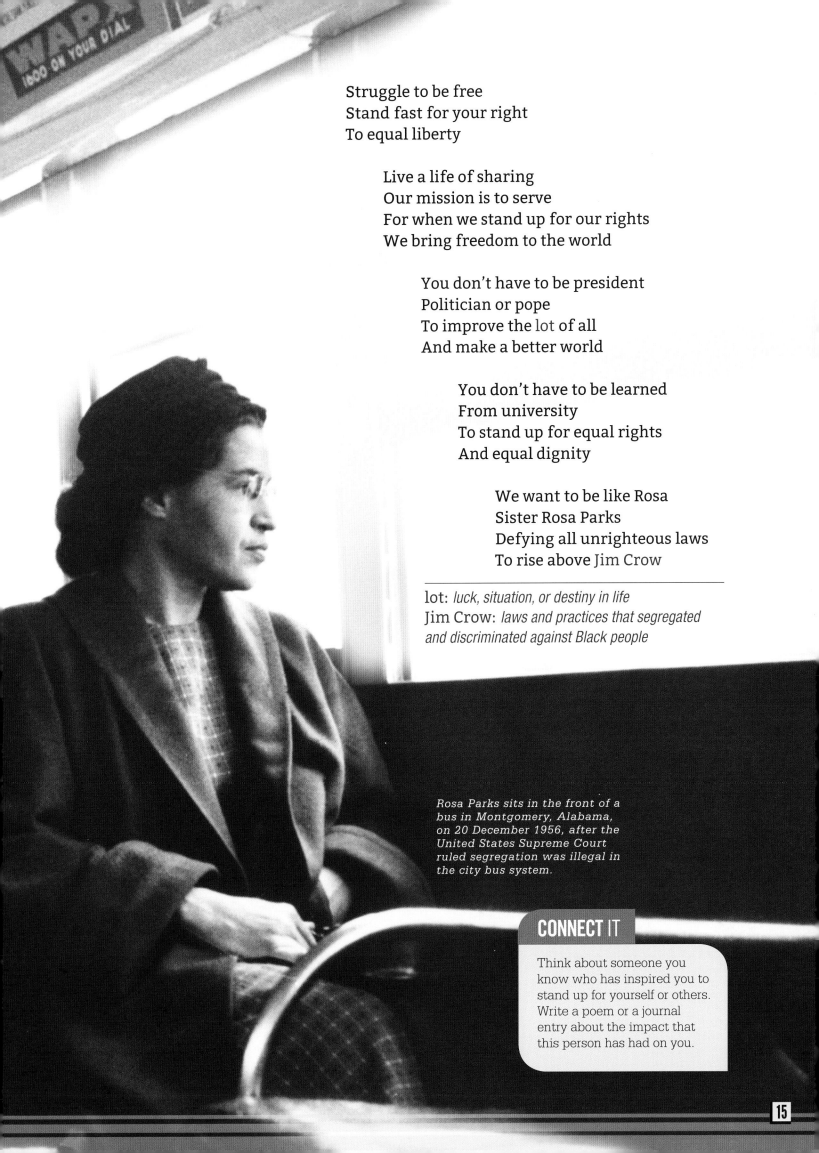

Struggle to be free
Stand fast for your right
To equal liberty

Live a life of sharing
Our mission is to serve
For when we stand up for our rights
We bring freedom to the world

You don't have to be president
Politician or pope
To improve the lot of all
And make a better world

You don't have to be learned
From university
To stand up for equal rights
And equal dignity

We want to be like Rosa
Sister Rosa Parks
Defying all unrighteous laws
To rise above Jim Crow

lot: *luck, situation, or destiny in life*
Jim Crow: *laws and practices that segregated and discriminated against Black people*

*Rosa Parks sits in the front of a bus in Montgomery, Alabama, on 20 December 1956, after the United States Supreme Court ruled segregation was illegal in the city bus system.*

## CONNECT IT

Think about someone you know who has inspired you to stand up for yourself or others. Write a poem or a journal entry about the impact that this person has had on you.

# Sitting Down and Standing Up for Your Rights

## THINK ABOUT IT

In a small group, talk about a time when you had to fight for your right to do something. Discuss the outcome of this situation.

**VIOLA DESMOND WAS** born in 1914 and raised in Halifax, Nova Scotia. She was a business person who owned a beauty parlour and barbershop with her husband, Jack. She also ran her own beauty school. Desmond is best known for challenging segregation in Nova Scotia. Read the following fictional narrative written in the voice of Desmond about a real event during which she fought against inequality.

> Why does the author choose to put the word "helpful" in quotation marks?

In the United States, I knew where I was or was not welcome. There were "helpful" signs all around that showed me which water fountain or public facilities I was allowed to use. But here, in Canada, it was more difficult to navigate the subtleties of racial discrimination. I guess you could say that I had to learn where I was not welcome the hard way.

This part of my story begins on a cold winter night in 1946 while I was on my way to Sydney, Nova Scotia. I don't recall the exact reason for my journey, but I remember that I was on business. Jack and I worked very hard to establish our beauty parlour and barbershop. It was important to us to also help other Black Nova Scotians. Being so busy, I found myself travelling all over Nova Scotia to make things happen for our company. Being successful is hard work, and I was committed to making our business successful. Nevertheless, life caught up with me, and on the way to my destination, my car broke down. Nothing could have prepared me for what happened later that evening.

I was in New Glasgow when I slowly made my way to a nearby garage. The mechanic assured me that the car could be fixed, but that it wouldn't be ready until the next day. As they say, when life gives you lemons, make lemonade. I signed the repair agreements and decided that the time waiting could be spent doing something that I very rarely had the opportunity to do — enjoying some much-needed time to myself. I thought I would browse the shops or have a bite to eat. As I strolled around town, I spotted the Roseland Theatre. It had been a while since I had last enjoyed a film. *The Dark Mirror* was showing. It wasn't necessarily my kind of film, but I thought it would do to pass the time.

As I stood in the queue to purchase my ticket, I thought about where I could get the best view. "One down, please," I announced to the cashier.

I reached into my handbag and took out a $1 bill to pay the 40 cents for the ticket. With my ticket in hand, I looked for a seat downstairs and waited for the film to start.

I reached the usher; however, instead of accepting my ticket, she looked at me and said, "This is an upstairs ticket; you will have to go upstairs." As she pointed to the balcony above, I saw patrons leering at me. I read my ticket, and sure enough, the cashier had given me a ticket for the balcony. I politely excused myself and headed back to the ticket booth to notify the cashier of her mistake. "Excuse me, ma'am," I announced. "It seems that you have given me the wrong ticket. I requested a lower-level seat, but I received a ticket for the balcony."

"I'm sorry, but I'm not permitted to sell downstairs tickets to you people," she said. *You people?* I was deeply offended. I looked around in disbelief — I didn't see any signs validating her claim. Angry and offended, I walked away. When the cashier began helping the next person in the queue, I re-entered the theatre and took a seat downstairs. The nerve. I could sit wherever I wanted. I requested a ticket

> What character traits do you think someone needs to stand up for his or her rights?

**As more people entered the downstairs section, I noticed that I could not spot any other Black patrons.**

and was willing to pay for its cost. It was not my fault the cashier would only issue me an upstairs ticket.

As more people entered the downstairs section, I noticed that I could not spot any other Black patrons. It was then that I heard whispers and felt glares piercing through the back of my neck. Soon afterwards, the usher approached me. "I told you to go upstairs." I refused to budge. The usher then went to get the theatre manager.

"Ma'am, you've already been told to go upstairs," the manager growled. He pointed to the back of my ticket to show me the theatre's right to refuse admission to whomever it wished. He told me to take my belongings and go up to the balcony if I wanted to see the movie.

"I never sit upstairs because I can't see very well from that distance," I asserted in my most confident tone. With my heart racing and my palms sweating, I fixed my gaze on the screen and waited for the film to begin.

The next thing I knew, I felt two strong hands gripping my shoulders, and I was dragged to the lobby. I thought that the manager was dragging me, but then I saw that it was another man. The man claimed that he was a police officer and shoved me into a police car. It all happened so fast. I didn't realize how serious the situation was until I was pushed into a jail cell with the door locked behind me.

"Always maintain your integrity," Momma used to tell me. So, I did. I straightened my clothes and hair, and then I sat down and waited. I waited and I waited, until one of the officers led me to the courthouse where the magistrate declared that I was being convicted of tax evasion. Tax evasion! They convicted me because they said I had not

paid the one-cent difference in tax between a balcony ticket and a downstairs ticket. That was not the issue whatsoever! I knew the truth and so did everyone else — they didn't want me sitting with the White patrons. They wanted me to "know my place." They could at least be honest about the situation, I remember thinking. But no, in the eyes of the court, this case was merely about tax evasion. What it was really about was the widespread racist culture that existed throughout Canada. We were not necessarily witness to it in words, but we observed it through actions. Ultimately, I was fined $26 for my "crime."

integrity: *quality of being honest and having strong morals*
magistrate: *head official of a court that handles minor offences*

## AN OFFICIAL APOLOGY

Viola Desmond's ordeal helped mobilize the African Canadian community to end racial discrimination in Nova Scotia. With the support of the Nova Scotia Association for the Advancement of Coloured People and Carrie Best, the founder of Nova Scotia's first African Canadian newspaper, the charges were fought and the conviction was dropped. However, it wasn't until 45 years after Desmond's death that justice was fully served. On 15 April 2010, the Lieutenant-Governor of Nova Scotia, Mayann Francis, used the Royal Prerogative of Mercy and granted Desmond the first-ever posthumous pardon in Canada. The government apologized for what she had experienced. Although Desmond never heard the apology, it serves as a reminder of her role in African Canadians' struggle for equality.

Royal Prerogative of Mercy: *power exercised by the Governor General or a Lieutenant-Governor of a province to grant leniency or a pardon*

posthumous: *occurring after death*

After an official apology from the Government of Nova Scotia, Lieutenant-Governor Mayann Francis signs the document granting a posthumous pardon to Desmond. Wanda Robson (left), Desmond's sister, attended the ceremony.

**CONNECT IT**

Write a journal entry about an event in your life for which you would want to be remembered. Direct your journal entry to an audience in the future. Include the character traits that you demonstrated in this situation. Explain why this event was important to you.

# DONALD WILLARD MOORE:

# CHANGING CANADA'S LAWS
## ONE LETTER AT A TIME

**PAM ARGUE**
*THE OAKVILLE BEAVER*
10 MARCH 2004

### THINK ABOUT IT

Multiculturalism is an official policy in Canada. Why do you think this is important?

**DONALD WILLARD MOORE** was a rights activist who had a huge impact on Canadian immigration laws. For 30 years, he fought against the discrimination in Canada's immigration policy. In 1962, Moore's efforts finally paid off. Racial origin was no longer used as a basis for immigration acceptance.

On 22 August 1994, Moore died at the age of 102. He left behind a legacy that changed the face of Canada. Read the following newspaper opinion piece to find out more about this inspirational man.

What words in this paragraph are evidence that this is an opinion piece?

Martin Luther King Jr. is a well-known Black American who played a major role in changing the way in which Black people are treated. A Canadian man who changed Canada's immigration laws was Donald Willard Moore. Unfortunately, most Canadians do not know who this courageous man was. It is time for that to change. I think this amazing Canadian deserves more recognition than he has been given. He set up the Negro Citizenship Association, and battled the immigration laws. Gandhi said, "A small group of determined spirits fired by an unquenchable faith in their mission can alter the course of history." Donald Moore and the Negro Citizenship Association did just that.

Donald Moore was born on 2 November 1891 in Barbados. He came to Canada in 1913 in search of a dream: a better life where he could receive the education denied to him by poverty in his birthplace. Donald declared Toronto was a great place to live in and quickly got a job as a tailor. Gazing down on King Street at the theatres, churches, and parks, he thought, "Here to the left of me is food for the body, on the right of me is food for the soul, and beyond is fun for relaxing."

Donald made many friends and became secretary of the Afro-Community Church of Canada. He opened up the gym of the church to the young Black people in the neighbourhood to use for roller skating, boxing, and other activities that were banned to them elsewhere because of the colour of their skin.

Customers, friends, and neighbours confided their problems to Donald. By 1950, a common problem was the unequal treatment of Black West Indians seeking entry to Canada. Immigrants were refused entry because of a law, which, according to the Toronto District Superintendent of Immigration, stated that "immigrants should be able readily to become adapted and integrated into the life of the Canadian community within a reasonable time after their entry." Government officials felt that West Indians would not be able to adapt to our cold climates within the specified time period or that they would become ill because of the cold and ultimately become a burden on society.

*Moore in 1992*

In 1951, Donald had a meeting with several nationals in his home. He explained to this group the actions of the Immigration Department in the many refusals of Black persons coming from the West Indies, the hardships and disappointments, the time and energy, and the money expended by people who could hardly afford it. Donald Moore suggested that they should make a determined effort to find out why Black West Indians were refused entry to Canada while White West Indians would enter without any difficulties. This was the beginning of what was to be known as the Negro Citizenship Association.

"We bring no sword, no gun, no explosive, our only weapon is that of reason, justice, and love. We know that you will give ear to our requests … our cause is just, and the love of mankind surmounts all difficulties." Donald Moore did not believe in violence, and he took up the battle against the cruel immigration laws with protests, letters, and more meetings of the Negro Citizenship Association.

On 27 April 1954, the Negro Citizenship Association sent a delegation to Ottawa to present a brief to the prime minister to protest sections in the *Immigration Act*. Under the act, Black British subjects in the Caribbean area were denied the same rights and privileges as White people. The brief was intended to show the harm these regulations caused and to seek changes.

surmounts: *overcomes*
delegation: *group of representatives*

We owe the way our country is now to Donald Moore.

In 1962, after hundreds of letters, Ottawa finally struck down the immigration ruling, which used racial origin as exclusionary and, by that action, changed the face of Canadian society.

We owe the way our country is now to Donald Moore. If he hadn't taken up his battle, … we would not have the knowledge and understanding of other cultures and religions as we do now. We would not have the famous Caribana and would not be the culturally diverse country we are today. When people talk about Martin Luther King Jr., I am going to talk about my Canadian Martin Luther, Donald Moore.

exclusionary: *leaving out*

How would Canada be different today if Moore and other rights activists had not succeeded in changing the immigration laws?

*The April/May 1954 edition of The Canadian Negro, which shows a picture of Moore (top left) and other delegates on their way to Ottawa*

*Moore (on right) with members of the Negro Citizenship Association*

## CONNECT IT

Immigration to Canada has not always been easy for certain groups of people. Choose one of the following Canadian immigration stories and find out what it might have been like for one of these groups to try to settle in Canada. Write an opinion piece on the story you choose.

- Chinese people after the construction of the Canadian Pacific Railway
- Caribbean women during the Caribbean Domestic Scheme
- South Asian people from India while the *Continuous Passage Act* was in effect

# FIGHTING for RIGHTS

What do you think about when you hear the words "protest" and "demonstration"? In your opinion, are these words negative or positive?

**WHEN INJUSTICES OCCUR,** it is important for people to stand up for their rights. In Canada, our rights are protected by the *Canadian Charter of Rights and Freedoms*. One Charter right is the freedom of peaceful assembly. This means that people across the country can meet to share their ideas with others. This is sometimes done through peaceful protests.

During most of Canada's history, African Canadians and other racialized groups have been forced to fight to get the same rights as others. Many protests were peaceful. However, others erupted in violence. In many cases, protests have led to positive change, making Canada a more inclusive, equitable country. Read the following case studies about some protests that are important in Canadian history.

equitable: *fair*

# SIR GEORGE WILLIAMS UNIVERSITY
## Montreal, Quebec

What would you do if you received a lower grade than you thought you deserved? In 1968, six African Canadian students at Sir George Williams University in Montreal knew what to do. They filed a formal complaint to the university about their biology professor. They believed that Perry Anderson was discriminating against them by not giving any Black student a grade better than a C. In response to their complaints, the university formed a committee to investigate. However, the students were unhappy with the university's choice of committee members.

Students organized sit-ins and handed out pamphlets to publicize their case of discrimination. On 29 January 1969, about 200 students occupied the university's computer lab for a peaceful sit-in. The sit-in lasted until 10 February when the protesters and the university thought they had reached an agreement. However, when the agreement fell through, things turned violent. The protesters threw computers out the windows and wrecked other property. They caused close to $2 million worth of damage.

Ninety-seven protesters were arrested. Of those arrested, 55 were White. Even though the majority of people arrested were White, the media focused on the arrests of the Black students.

The event caused the university to analyze how to handle complaints of racism. In 1971, a new process was developed that involved students in decision-making at the university.

Roosevelt "Rosie" Douglas, who was considered to be the leader of the 1969 protest, went on to become the prime minister of his home country of Dominica. Anne Cools, born in Barbados, who was another participant in the protest, later became the first Black person to be appointed to the Canadian Senate.

---

sit-ins: *protests where a group of people occupy a place*

*Sir George Williams University joined with Loyola College in 1974 to form Concordia University.*

*Aftermath of the largest student uprising in Canadian history*

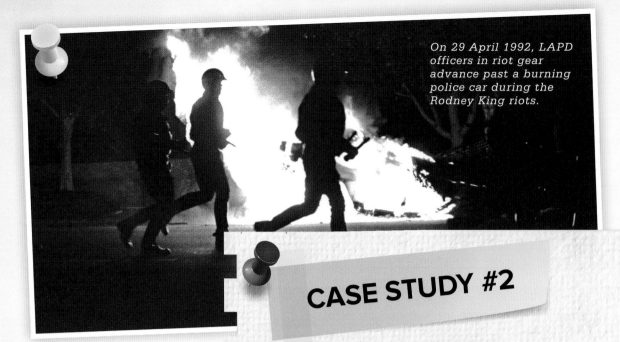

*On 29 April 1992, LAPD officers in riot gear advance past a burning police car during the Rodney King riots.*

# YONGE STREET
## Toronto, Ontario

On 29 April 1992, the now-infamous trial of the police officers who had beaten Rodney King ended in Los Angeles, California. After a high-speed chase the year before, King had been pulled over by White officers and brutally beaten. An amateur cameraperson caught the incident on video. The officers faced assault charges; however, a mainly White jury acquitted them. The decision sparked mass protests and riots in Los Angeles and resulted in dozens of deaths. Many Canadians were also outraged by this verdict. Just days after the Los Angeles protests began, a 22-year-old Black man was shot and killed by Toronto police. Raymond Lawrence was just one victim in a string of police shootings of Black men in the Toronto region at the time. On 4 May 1992, Lawrence's death, along with the verdict in the King case, ignited a large protest on Yonge Street in Toronto against police violence. The protest grew to include approximately 1000 people. It began peacefully, and several of the protesters did not turn to violence to have their voices heard. However, as the crowd grew, some of the protesters became disruptive, and around 30 people were arrested.

Following the protest, the Government of Ontario released a report on race relations. The investigation concluded that systemic racism against minorities existed in the region, especially against African Canadians. The protest and the report led to an expansion of the province's anti-racism department, the introduction of employment equity legislation, and an increase in funding for community development projects.

*Rodney King*

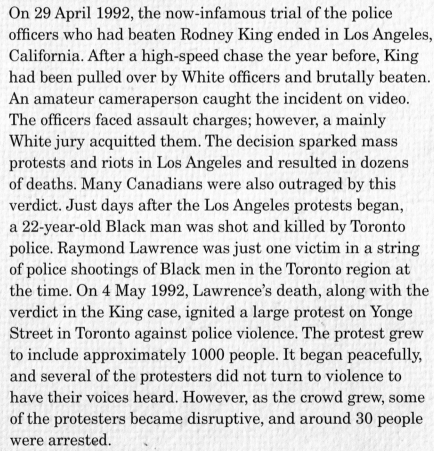

systemic: *relating to the patterns, policies, and practices of a system*

# AGRICULTURE WORKERS ALLIANCE
## Toronto, Ontario

Every year, thousands of people come to Canada to work in the agriculture industry. Many leave spouses and children in their home country. In December 2012, the Canadian government eliminated some benefits that foreign migrant workers received as part of Employment Insurance (EI). Seasonal workers who took time off to take care of newborns or sick children no longer received a portion of their pay.

*UFCW Canada and AWA workers during the launch of the "Migrant Workers Are Parents Too" campaign*

"These workers are proud parents who sacrifice a tremendous amount to provide for their families, and to make Canada's agriculture industry possible," said Wayne Hanley, the then national president of the United Food and Commercial Workers (UFCW Canada) Union.

In protest, UFCW Canada and the Agriculture Workers Alliance (AWA) exercised their freedom of peaceful assembly. On 14 June 2013, which was Father's Day, the UFCW and the AWA organized a campaign called "Migrant Workers Are Parents Too." Migrant workers and their supporters gathered at the office of Diane Finley, the Minister of Human Resources and Skills Development at that time. This department was responsible for EI and the programs that bring migrant and temporary workers to Canada. Across Canada, migrant workers from Mexico and the Caribbean also gathered at AWA support centres. Unfortunately, these protests did not change the government's decision.

Human Resources and Skills Development is now known as Employment and Social Development.

---

migrant workers: *people who move from place to place to find work*

*Migrant workers from Mexico and the Caribbean*

## CONNECT IT

Use the Web and other resources to learn about other protests in Canada. For example, you could start by looking at the Idle No More protests. Choose one event, and write a case study about it like those that you read about in this text.

# BROMLEY ARMSTRONG:

## NOT A SECOND-CLASS CITIZEN

> Unions are organizations that help protect workers' rights.

> Do you think that the labour union should have helped Armstrong even if he hadn't attended any of its meetings? Why or why not?

**THE WORK OF** civil rights leader Bromley Armstrong helped many people who experienced discrimination at work and in other public places. Learn about him in this profile.

Bromley Armstrong was born in Jamaica in 1926. He came to Canada in 1947 and began working at the Massey-Harris plant, a farm equipment manufacturer in Ontario. Unhappy with his job, Armstrong applied for a welding position. His application never received a response. When he followed up, Armstrong was told that his application had been misplaced, so he reapplied. He applied three times, but his application kept getting "lost."

It became clear to Armstrong that because of racism, people of colour could not get certain jobs. Armstrong turned to the plant's union for help. However, the president of the union pointed out that Armstrong had never attended any union meetings. Armstrong accepted that he couldn't just ask the union for help when he needed it. He had to get involved, so he became determined to attend every meeting from then on. He realized he needed to be a presence and a voice for himself and other people of colour. This experience marked the beginning of Armstrong's five decades of civil rights activism.

Armstrong did not face discrimination only at work. In the 1940s and 1950s, although Ontario was becoming increasingly racially diverse, many hotels, clubs, and restaurants refused to serve African Canadians. However, even though racial discrimination was common at this time in Canada, it was difficult to prove. Armstrong, along with a team of other civil rights activists, worked to prove its existence. They collected evidence by going to businesses that were known for refusing service to people of colour.

With this evidence and by persistently lobbying the Ontario government, they were ultimately successful in their fight for change. Premier Leslie Frost, of Ontario, enacted two laws that eventually changed the face of Canada's civil rights practices. The first was the *Fair Employment Practices Act*, which outlawed discrimination in places of employment. The second was the *Fair Accommodation Practices Act*, which prohibited businesses from discriminating against customers. The creation of these laws was a victory for Armstrong and other people of colour in Ontario.

Armstrong was also the founder of many organizations, including the Jamaican Canadian Association, the Urban Alliance on Race Relations, the Toronto Black Business and Professional Association, and the Canadian Ethnocultural Council. In recognition of his work and dedication as a civil rights activist, Armstrong was named a Member of the Order of Ontario and a Member of the Order of Canada. These honours are given to people for their work in improving the lives of Ontarians and Canadians.

On 11 June 2013, York University awarded Armstrong an honorary degree for his "dedication, passion, and lifelong commitment to the battle against racism." Because of Armstrong, laws now protect people in Ontario from being treated as second-class citizens.

*Hand-drawn portrait of Armstrong*

## IT BECAME CLEAR TO ARMSTRONG THAT BECAUSE OF RACISM, PEOPLE OF COLOUR COULD NOT GET CERTAIN JOBS.

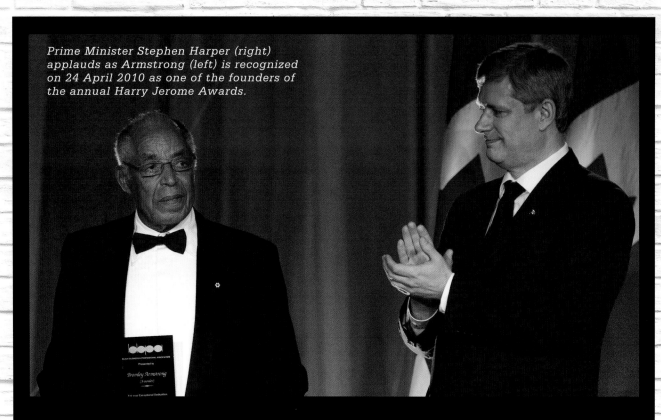

Prime Minister Stephen Harper (right) applauds as Armstrong (left) is recognized on 24 April 2010 as one of the founders of the annual Harry Jerome Awards.

# THESE ARE JUST A FEW HIGHLIGHTS OF ARMSTRONG'S REMARKABLE LIFE.

**1951:** Named a Toronto District Soccer League all-star

**1973:** Began publishing *The Islander*, a newspaper dedicated to the Black and West Indian communities of Toronto

**1975:** Started working for five years as a commissioner for the Ontario Human Rights Commission

**1998:** Presented with the Harmony Award for educating individuals, organizations, and communities through his commitment to human rights, race relations, and labour relations in Canada

**2000:** Published his memoir, *Bromley: Tireless Champion for Just Causes*

**2004:** Had an annual human rights award (the Bromley Armstrong award) created in his honour by the Toronto & York Region Labour Council

## CONNECT IT

Imagine you are a business owner writing a "Help Wanted" advertisement to describe your business and the requirements needed for a job. In your advertisement, explain how and why your company encourages diversity. You may want to look at other advertisements for examples.

# RACIAL PROFILING

A group of protesters in Toronto

## THINK ABOUT IT

How could you support someone who is being discriminated against because of his or her race?

**IMAGINE BEING ACCUSED** of something you didn't do just because of the colour of your skin. Unfortunately, this happens often. It's called racial profiling.

Racial profiling happens when a person is seen as a threat to the safety or security of the public based on stereotypes about him or her rather than on reasonable suspicions. Because of this, racialized groups are often watched more closely and critically than others, even though they have not done anything wrong.

Racial profiling is a form of discrimination. It can happen in different ways. Sometimes, people are discriminated against by the police and the courts. Other times, they may experience racial discrimination in the customer service industry. In this industry, racial profiling happens when people are ignored, refused service, followed in a store, physically searched, or wrongfully detained because of their race. It also happens when salespeople question whether shoppers can or cannot afford something based on their race.

In 2013, the Nova Scotia Human Rights Commission released the results of a survey from the Consumer Racial Profiling Project. The survey compared how White, Asian, African Canadian, Middle Eastern, Aboriginal, and Latin American people were treated in the service industry. The results of the survey showed that "race or ethnicity is the most significant factor in the experience of consumer incidents when compared to other demographics, such as age, gender, and level of education." The responses of Aboriginal people and African Canadians showed that they were among those who are most often discriminated against.

Read the following reader's theatre script, which is based on a number of real events, for an example of how racial profiling takes place in Canada.

## CHARACTERS:

- Narrator 1
- Narrator 2
- Felicity
- Sandy
- Store clerk
- Security guard
- Mr. Wilson

**Narrator 1:** Fifteen-year-old Felicity is adjusting to her new life in Brandon, Manitoba. But being the only Black student in her school isn't easy. In Montreal, her school was very diverse.

**Narrator 2:** After six months in Brandon, Felicity has surrounded herself with a great group of friends. However, just when she starts to feel accepted in her new community, something terrible happens …

**Felicity:** Guess what? I've finally saved up enough money to buy a new pair of jeans! I've been wanting them for months, but my parents wouldn't buy them for me. They said paying $100 for a pair of jeans was a waste of money. They just don't get it …

**Sandy:** That's great! And we wear the same size, so I can borrow them. I bet my brown leather belt would go perfectly with them.

**Felicity:** Ha ha, OK. Meet me at your locker after school. We can head to the mall together.

**Sandy:** Sounds like a plan.

**Narrator 1:** Once afternoon classes end, Sandy and Felicity meet at Sandy's locker.

**Narrator 2:** A half hour later, they arrive at the store's entrance.

**Felicity:** Let's make this quick. This store gives me the creeps. I don't like being here. But I *really* want those jeans!

**Sandy:** You don't like it here? I shop here with my sister all the time. It's great!

**Felicity:** I don't know. It's just *creepy*. Nobody ever greets me or smiles at me. Nobody helps me find what I'm looking for. I feel ignored. Last time I was here, the salesperson even followed me around the store. It was really strange.

**Sandy:** Weird! I haven't noticed that before.

**Felicity:** I almost get the feeling it's because I'm Black.

**Sandy:** You think that people who work here treat you differently because you're Black? I'm sure you're just overreacting. Canada is a multicultural country.

**Felicity:** You're probably right …

**Narrator 1:** Felicity and Sandy enter the store.

**Store clerk:** Welcome to our store, ladies. Is there something I can help you with?

**Sandy (*whispering to Felicity*):** See. I told you this place is OK.

**Narrator 2:** Sandy picks up a sweater she likes on a nearby table.

**Sandy:** Oh, this is nice.

**Store clerk:** That would look lovely on you. I can bring it to the change room for you.

**Sandy:** Actually, we're here for my friend. She is looking to buy the jeans on the shelf over there.

**Narrator 1:** The store clerk watches Felicity shop out of the corner of her eye. Moments later, Felicity walks over to the store clerk.

**Felicity:** You don't seem to have a size 8. Can you please check if you have any more?

**Store clerk:** Oh, the ones with the stitching down the leg are really expensive. Maybe too expensive. Let me show you some similar ones that don't cost as much.

**Felicity:** With all due respect, ma'am, I didn't ask you the price. Can you please check if you have any more size 8s?

**Narrator 2:** The store clerk goes to the stockroom to search for more pairs of jeans.

**Narrator 1:** Soon afterwards, a security guard enters the store.

**Felicity (*to Sandy*):**
See what I mean? That security guard is watching my every move.

**Sandy:** Actually, it really looks like he is. That's so unfair!

**Narrator 2:** The store clerk returns with the pair of jeans and reluctantly gives them to Felicity.

**Felicity:** I'll take them.

**Store clerk:** Just so that you know, we don't have a layaway program at this store. We only take cash, debit, or credit.

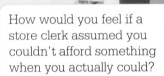

**Felicity:** Excuse me? I didn't ask about a layaway program. I'd like to put them on my debit card.

**Narrator 1:** The security guard looks at Felicity and then back at the store clerk.

**Security guard (*to store clerk*):**
Is everything OK here?

**Felicity (*quietly*):**
Here we go again …

**Felicity (*to store clerk*):**
You know what? I'm really sick of being treated this way in your store. I don't need these jeans. And I definitely don't need to be treated like a criminal.

**Sandy:** Let's get out of here.

**Narrator 2:** Felicity returns home and looks up the contact information for the store's head office on her computer. She writes an email about her experience at the store and how it made her feel. She includes her phone number and sends it off to the contact person at the head office.

**Narrator 1:** The following day, Felicity is at home when she hears her phone ring. She answers the call.

How would you feel if a store clerk assumed you couldn't afford something when you actually could?

**Felicity:** Hello?

**Mr. Wilson:** Hello, Felicity. My name is Jerry Wilson, and I am the manager of customer relations at Jean World. I am calling to let you know that we received your email and that we are very happy that you wrote to us. What you went through yesterday should not have happened, and we want you to know that we will be conducting a thorough investigation into this matter.

**Felicity:** I'm happy to hear that.

**Mr. Wilson:** It is our goal to make all of our customers feel welcome in our stores. No one should be treated as you were. I assure you that this issue will be handled quickly. We do hope that you will continue to shop at our store. You are a valued client.

**Felicity:** I will have to give it some thought, but thank you for looking into this.

**Mr. Wilson:** As an apology from our company, we would like to ship you a free pair of the jeans you discussed in your email.

**Felicity:** Oh, wow! That would be great! Thank you very much.

**Mr. Wilson:** You're welcome. Thank you again for letting us know about your experience. I hope you have a wonderful day.

**Felicity:** No problem! I hope you have a great day, too.

## CONNECT IT

In a group, write an alternative ending to the script that shows another way that Felicity could have challenged how she was treated in the store. Present your script to the class.

# TAMARA GORDON
## URGES YOUTH TO
# AIM HIGH

**RON FANFAIR**
*SHARE NEWS*
30 MAY 2013

## THINK ABOUT IT

What are some obstacles that you have had to face on your way to accomplishing a goal? How did you overcome those obstacles?

**AS A YOUNG** person, Tamara Gordon, of Ontario, was an athlete with a passion for sports. But in 2002, her life changed drastically. She was severely injured in a skiing accident and was left partially paralyzed and requiring the use of a wheelchair. Despite this huge obstacle, Gordon continues to pursue her dreams.

Gordon created the Tamara Gordon Foundation. The foundation helps to protect the rights of people with disabilities and to empower them to improve their lives. The foundation believes that people with disabilities have the right to contribute to society without facing discrimination, to become self-sufficient, and to access the services and accommodations they need.

Gordon's foundation raises awareness of the issues facing people with disabilities. It targets barriers in society that prevent people with disabilities from accessing opportunities that are available to others. It encourages an understanding and respectful dialogue about disability issues.

Read the following article to learn how Gordon inspires young people.

# "Before that day, I was sailing on the ocean of life **smoothly and confidently.** "

Life is filled with obstacles and frustrations. How you handle the challenges could determine your altitude.

That was Tamara Gordon's message to Malvern Christian Assembly elementary and high-school graduates last Sunday night. ...

Gordon suffered a debilitating spinal cord injury in February 2002 while on a high-school downhill skiing trip. The spinal cord and brachial injuries left her paralyzed from the waist down and without the use of her dominant left hand.

"Before that day, I was sailing on the ocean of life smoothly and confidently," she told the young people. "The sun was shining on me, and everything seemed to be working in my favour. It was a time when I was walking and running like all of you. As a small child, my dream had always been to win a basketball scholarship in the United States and pursue a law degree. Just three days after speaking with the scouts and thinking that my dreams were going to become a reality once I graduated from high school, I had this accident."

---

debilitating: *disabling; damaging*
brachial: *relating to the arm*

> Do you think this sentence is an effective metaphor? Why or why not?

Tamara Gordon was paralyzed from the waist down and lost the use of one of her arms after a skiing accident.

> ""My body was paralyzed, **but my mind was not.** I refused to use paralysis as an excuse to stop achieving." ""

Gordon graduated from York University with honours.

Despite the setback, the Markham resident graduated on time from high school as an Ontario scholar with a 91 percent average.

Four years ago, she completed her undergraduate degree at York University in Administrative Studies and was on the Dean's List.

In spite of limited mobility, recurring health issues, and challenges associated with functioning as a student and a person with disabilities, Gordon was quite active on campus. She headed the student caucus for undergraduates with disabilities and served as the student undergraduate representative for Access York.

"When I had my accident, I was immediately faced with a choice," she said. "I could give up and accept defeat, or I could choose to continue to fight and to live life to the best of my ability. I think you can guess what I decided to do just by my presence here today. My body was paralyzed, but my mind was not. I refused to use paralysis as an excuse to stop achieving."

Gordon is the recipient of close to 60 scholarships, certificates, and awards, including Harry Jerome and TD Canada Trust scholarships. In August 2006, she completed an internship at a TD bank close to her then Don Mills residence and was offered a full-time position. She currently works with a branch near her Markham residence and is its diversity committee representative.

In 2009, she was the recipient of the Ontario Medal for Young Volunteers and the Mildred Theobalds Prize. ... The award was set up to honour the late long-time York University program coordinator.

caucus: *group of people with similar concerns*

*Gordon with former Ontario Lieutenant-Governor David Onley*

Gordon is also quite busy in the community. She sponsors a volunteer centre for the tenants in the Don Mills building where her mother still resides, and she's a board member on the Operating Engineers Local 793 Non-Profit Housing Inc. In the past, she was a peer support volunteer with the Canadian Paraplegic Association, spending hours with young people suffering from spinal cord injuries. She also spearheads a teen volunteer program and tutoring service, organizes free back-to-school barbecues and Canada Day celebrations, and presents motivational speeches, always reminding young people to strive to overcome barriers they face in life.

"My message to you tonight is simple," said Gordon. "Having determined your goals, I urge you to maintain your focus on them at all times and work hard. I promise that if you do this, you will accomplish whatever you desire because anything is possible. The difficulties and challenges are going to come because they are part of life."

The recipient of a Queen's Diamond Jubilee Medal from Prince Charles a year ago, Gordon recently set up a foundation to help young people realize their dreams. …

## CONNECT IT

Think of someone you know who is an inspiration like Gordon. Design a poster about this person, showing how he or she inspires others. Share your poster in a small group.

# WORDS of a HERO

## THINK ABOUT IT

Many people consider the late Nelson Mandela a hero. Think about what makes a person a hero. Who is your hero?

**NELSON MANDELA WAS** the first Black president of South Africa. He was also the country's first democratically elected president. His road to office wasn't an easy one. He spent 27 years in prison for fighting against Apartheid in South Africa. Mandela died in 2013.

Mandela was a hero to people around the world because of the courage and wisdom he demonstrated as a leader and a freedom fighter. The following quotations are examples of the wisdom he brought to the struggle in South Africa.

democratically: *chosen by the people through voting*

Nelson Mandela

"Education is the most powerful weapon which you can use to change the world."

What is one example of how you can use your education to change the world?

"I learned that courage was not the absence of fear, but the triumph over it. The brave man is not he who does not feel afraid, but he who conquers that fear."

"During my lifetime, I have dedicated myself to this struggle of the African people. I have fought against White domination, and I have fought against Black domination. I have cherished the ideal of a democratic and free society in which all persons live together in harmony and with equal opportunities. It is an ideal which I hope to live for and to achieve. But if needs be, it is an ideal for which I am prepared to die."

"Everyone can rise above their circumstances and achieve success if they are dedicated to and passionate about what they do."

"Since my release, I have become more convinced than ever that the real makers of history are the ordinary men and women of our country; their participation in every decision about the future is the only guarantee of true democracy and freedom."

"It always seems impossible until it's done."

"I hate race discrimination most intensely and in all its manifestations. I have fought it all during my life; I fight it now, and will do so until the end of my days."

manifestations: *actions, events, or objects that clearly reveal something*

CONNECT IT

Choose one quotation by Nelson Mandela. It can be from this book, or you can find one on your own. Make a collage that includes the quotation and some images that you find. Show your collage to another student. Explain why you chose the quotation and the images you did.

# How Can *You* Make a *Difference?*

**THINK ABOUT IT**

Think about an issue in your school or community. What are some things that you can do to influence change and make a difference?

**IN CANADA, WE** are lucky enough to have our rights protected by the *Canadian Charter of Rights and Freedoms*. However, around the world, people still face human rights violations. Read on to find out what you can do to make a difference in your community and around the world.

## Sign a Petition or Create Your Own!

In order to have a major impact on an issue that matters to you, you need the support of as many people as possible. A good way to get support is to start a petition and get signatures from people who believe in your cause. The more signatures a petition gets, the greater the chance that it will be taken seriously by governments or officials related to the cause.

When creating your own petition, make sure you provide information about the cause and the difference you're hoping to make. A good place to start is to answer the 5 Ws and H: What would you like to see changed? When and where is this issue occurring? Why do you think this issue is important? Who are you directing your petition toward? How would you like change to occur?

There are many websites that allow you to search for a petition that already exists. One of the most popular petition websites is change.org. This website allows users to sign petitions as well as create their own. A petition started by Holly Jarrett of Cornwall, Ontario, aims to bring awareness to the status of missing or murdered Aboriginal women in Canada. The petition has over 328 000 signatures and even got a response from Kellie Leitch, the Minister of Status of Women.

# Volunteer

There are many ways you can volunteer your time and effort to help those in your community and around the world.

Search online for organizations that help those in need. You could volunteer your time by handing out flyers for a human rights conference or by helping set up the event.

There are many benefits to becoming a volunteer. Volunteering allows you to become a more active member of your community. When you help those in your community, you are helping your community grow. Both you and your community benefit when you give back and volunteer. Volunteering can also help you learn new skills.

Some people even volunteer in other countries. International organizations such as the United Nations send volunteers around the world. The goal of the United Nations Volunteers (UNV) program is to achieve human rights for all.

## Attend a Protest

Protests bring people together to make sure their voices are heard. Many protests take place near or outside a building or an area that has particular significance to a cause. Some examples of places people protest include government buildings, television and media stations, and large, central locations in a city or town.

One of the biggest benefits of a protest is that it forces government leaders and those in power to pay attention. When a protest happens, media outlets will cover it on news programs and websites, bringing awareness about the cause not only to officials, but also to the general public.

When you attend a protest, make sure you are not by yourself and that you are with someone you trust. If a protest becomes too large or the people at the protest become too passionate about the cause, violence can sometimes erupt. Make sure you have a plan in place in case that happens. Protests should always be peaceful, and you should not associate with a protest or organization that promotes violence. You want people to pay attention to the cause, not to the violence.

## Write a Letter

Writing a letter to government officials, newspaper editors, television producers, business owners, and community leaders is another way to bring awareness to your cause. Make sure the people you address in your letter are those who will have the most impact on your cause. A community leader may be able to help change an issue in your community, but it would be more difficult for that person to make a difference to a global cause without the help of others.

If your cause has a specific organization associated with it, you can check the organization's website for tips on who would be best person to address your letter to. Some websites may even offer letter templates to help you get started. The more people you reach out to with your letter, the more awareness you will bring to your cause.

## Raise Awareness Online

Social media and online communities make it easier than ever to spread a message. One way to share a message is to start a blog or website. A blog or website can be easily shared with many people, making it one of the simplest ways to raise awareness about a cause.

Social media sites also offer great ways of promoting an issue online. When writing about a cause online, make sure you have up-to-date and accurate information. If you want to educate people about an issue, you want them to see you as an expert, so accuracy counts.

One goal of any online campaign should be to make a cause go "viral." This means having it spread rapidly so that it is seen by a large number of people.

## Fundraise or Donate

Organizations need not only your time but also your financial assistance. You can help by fundraising in your community or by donating directly to an organization.

There are many ways you can raise money for a cause. You could have a bake sale or hold a garage sale. The possibilities are endless! A fundraiser is a great opportunity to educate people about an issue. People can learn about where their money is going and how it helps the cause.

Other examples of fundraising events you can organize include talent shows, raffles, car washes, and neighbourhood sidewalk sales. If you are planning an event at your school, make sure that you have the approval of your teacher. Many schools have fundraising programs already in place. Some schools fundraise for organizations like the Heart and Stroke Foundation and the Terry Fox Foundation.

### CONNECT IT

Which of the strategies in these short reports would be your first choice for promoting human rights? Create a chart outlining the benefits and challenges of this strategy. In a small group, share your chart with your classmates.

# Index

# Acknowledgements

The publisher gratefully acknowledges the following for permission to reprint copyrighted material in this book.

Argue, Pamela. "Changing Canada's Laws One Letter at a Time," first published in The Oakville Beaver, 10 March 2004. Permission courtesy of the author.

Fanfair, Ron. "Paraplegic Urges Youth to Refuse to Let Obstacles Hinder Aspirations," from Share, posted on 30 May 2013. Permission courtesy of Share Publishing Inc.

"Strive to Be Like Rosa," by Charles Roach from Rhapso Prosodies: The Poetry and Paintings of Charles 'Mende' Roach. © Charles Roach 2012, A Different Publisher. Permission courtesy of Dawn Roach Bowen on behalf of the author's estate.

**Photo Sources**
**Cover:** hands–AJP/Shutterstock.com; **4:** [wave–Shiny Designer; justice scale–Jerry Sliwowski] Shutterstock.com; **6:** [paper–LeksusTuss; stripes–madpixblue; parliament–Denis Roger] Shutterstock.com; **7:** Charter of Rights–Library and Archives Canada; family–Andresr/Shutterstock.com; **8:** demonstrators–Everett Collection / SuperStock; **9:** entrance–Annette Kurylo; **10:** [texture–Ozerina Anna; background–HorenkO; leaves–paprika] Shutterstock.com; Viola Desmond–Marsha Barrow Smith/Black History Portraits; **11:** maple leaf–vectorOK/Shutterstock.com; Fair Employment Practices Act–iStockphoto.com/© shaunl; **12:** Pierre Trudeau–Harry Palmer Photographs/ A Portrait of Canada; **13:** Michaëlle Jean–Photo by Andrew Francis Wallace/ Toronto Star via Getty Images; **14:** Rosa Parks–© Bettmann/CORBIS; Charles Roach–Toronto Star / GetStock.com; **16:** illustrations–Megan Little; **21:** background–Lurin/Shutterstock.com; apology–THE CANADIAN PRESS/ Andrew Vaughan; **22:** paper background–Ice-Storm/Shutterstock.com; **23:** Donald Willard Moore–Andrew Stawicki / GetStock.com; words–GalaStudio/Shutterstock.com; **24:** Negro Citizenship Association–City of Toronto Archives; **25:** The Canadian Negro–City of Toronto Archives; **26:** background–BrAt82; placard–photka] Shutterstock.com; **27:** [paper–My Life Graphic; tags–rizvan3d] Shutterstock.com; Sir George Williams University–Fonds Conrad Poirier; building damage–Concordia University Records Management and Archives; **28:** riot–a katz/Shutterstock.com; Rodney King–Justin Hoch; **29:** [protesters; workers]–courtesy of UFCW Canada; **30:** bricks–Vladitto/Shutterstock.com; **31:** frame–Picsfive/Shutterstock.com; Bromley Armstrong–Portrait by Christian Elden (christianelden.com)/Black History Portraits; **32:** Harper & Bromley–THE CANADIAN PRESS/Chris Young; **33:** texture–Eky Studio/Shutterstock.com; protesters–Rene Johnston / Toronto Star; **34:** mall girls–Peter M. Fisher/CORBIS/Glowimages.com; **36:** jeans–fiphoto/Shutterstock.com; **38:** texture–RoyStudio.eu/Shutterstock.com; 39: graduation picture–courtesy of Tamara Gordon; **40:** Tamara Gordon–Rick Madonik / GetStock.com; **41:** Onley & Gordon–courtesy of Tamara Gordon; **42:** wall–Sergey Nivens/Shutterstock.com; Mandela–© Hans Gedda/Sygma/ Corbis; **44:** background–Toria/Shutterstock.com; **45:** volunteers–Monkey Business Images/Shutterstock.com; **46:** protest–Eric Crama/Shutterstock.com; pen holder–Seregam/Shutterstock.com; **47:** [mouse–cosma; donations–albund] Shutterstock.com; iPad–iStockphoto.com/© hanibaram.